THE WAY OF THE SEEKER

A Guide for Growth, Change, and Clarity

T.L. HURD

First published by Vital Expansion LLC. 2026

ISBN: 979-8-9944700-0-8

First edition

Contents

Foreword

For every soul brave enough to begin and
wise enough to trust that the way forward
reveals itself one step at a time.

Prologue

The moment arrives quietly. What once felt safe now feels suffocating. Familiar places turn strange. The road you've been traveling suddenly points toward a destination you no longer want to reach.

This is not a crisis. It's a call.

You might feel it as restlessness, a stirring in the quiet hours when distractions fall away. You might recognize it as a question that won't stop asking itself. Is this all there is? You might experience it as a door closing, forcing you to find another way forward.

However it arrives, the call is an invitation to transformation. It is a scent you suddenly recognize, warm amber and cedar, wafting through a door you've never noticed before. It is a pull that feels like a memory of a place you've never been. Not the kind that changes your circumstances, but the kind that changes you. It asks you to see past the layers of programming, expectations, and fear.

The gates are not physical places. They are thresholds of awareness, portals where you see yourself and your life with sudden clarity.

Each gate has a key made not of metal, but of insight. Each passage has an anchor. Not a magical object, but a reminder of what you've learned and who you're becoming.

The path is not easy. Transformation never is. But it is worth it. Every step. Every struggle. Every moment of doubt gives way to clarity.

You are reading this because you're ready. The restlessness has found you. The call has come. The first gate is opening.

Transformation does not begin with action.
It begins with awareness.

* * *

THE GIFTS OF TRANSFORMATION

As you journey through the gates, you can expect to gain:

Enhanced Self-Awareness - Discover deeper truths about yourself. The journey prompts you to explore your thoughts, emotions, and behaviors, allowing you to recognize patterns that may have gone unnoticed.

Improved Relationships - As you become more authentic and self-aware, your interactions with others will shift. You'll learn to communicate more openly and connect with others on a deeper level, paving the way for more meaningful relationships.

Greater Fulfillment - Through this process, you will uncover the passions and values that truly resonate with you. Following your unique path will lead to a more fulfilling life, one that is aligned with your authentic self.

Resilience and Growth - Transformation is not just about reaching a destination. It's about cultivating resilience. You will learn to navigate challenges with grace, embracing change and uncertainty as opportunities for growth.

Empowerment - By the end of this journey, you'll feel empowered to make choices that reflect your true desires and values. You'll have the tools to create a life that inspires you and aligns with your true purpose.

Introduction

This manuscript is a map of transformation. A field guide for those who sense there's more to life and are ready to discover it.

Not a prescription, but a reflection. Not a set of rules, but a record of my journey through six gates of awakening. Six keys found along the way that unlock what was always there. Six passages that shifted from confusion to clarity, fear to courage, survival to living fully.

I offer this not as someone who has all the answers, but as someone who has walked through fire and emerged changed. What you hold in your hands is both personal testimony and universal pattern. My story, yes, but also the story that lives in every human heart that longs for something more.

The journey begins with a call you can no longer ignore. It moves through doubt and discovery. It involves letting go and taking hold. It breaks down and builds up. It ends not with arrival, but with return. Coming home to yourself with new eyes and an open heart.

This is not a story about finding something outside yourself. It's about remembering what was always within you. Not about becoming someone new, but about uncovering who you've always been.

Each gate represents a passage, a threshold you must cross to move deeper into your own becoming. Some gates will feel familiar the moment you encounter them. Others will challenge everything you thought you knew about yourself. All of them are necessary.

At each gate, you'll discover a key that allows entrance. These keys represent moments of clarity, insights that unlock the next passage. Some are anchor objects. Physical items that open mental pathways when needed. The anchors are important to hold on to as you journey through each passage. They remind you of practices that help you, especially during tough times. A stone. A photograph. A scent. Even a specific texture that allows you to recall what you need in the moment. Whatever grounds you in truth when doubt creeps in. Collect them. Honor them. They will serve you long after you've moved through the gates.

Throughout this journey, I've learned that we are not alone in this work. There is something larger than ourselves moving through all things. Some call it God. Some call it the Universe, the Tao, Source, or simply Life itself. I don't claim to know its name or nature, but I have felt its presence. When we connect with our true selves, we tap into a current that has flowed long before us and will continue flowing after we're gone.

This is not about religion or doctrine. It's about acknowledging that we are part of something greater. When we say yes to our own transformation, wisdom that exceeds our understanding meets us. You can trust this. When you feel most alone or uncertain, remember there is a force at work that responds to your desire to grow.

I won't pretend this journey is easy. There were moments I wanted to turn back, to return to the comfortable numbness of my old life. Some days, I wondered if the call was real or just a fleeting feeling.

Here's what I know now. Once you've heard the call and glimpsed the possibility of who you might become, you can never completely ignore or forget it. The awareness has been planted. The seed has been sown. The only question is whether you'll water it or let it wither.

This manuscript is not a guarantee of where you'll end up. It's a companion for the journey. Use it as you need it. Read it straight through or return to specific gates when you need their wisdom. Mark the pages. Write in the margins. Make it yours.

The transformation that awaits you is one of a kind. Your gates may look different from mine.

Your keys may arrive in unexpected forms. Your anchors may be things I have never encountered. That's exactly as it should be.

What matters is that you begin. That you trust the stirring in your soul. Step through the first gate with courage and curiosity. Trust that everything you need will be revealed as you go.

You are ready for this. Even if you don't feel ready. Even if you're terrified. Even if you have no idea where this will lead.

The journey is calling you. Will you answer?

I

The Call

The first sign is always restlessness. What starts as a whisper in the space between sleep and waking. Turns into an inner stirring so profound that it raises questions about the life you are living. It's a persistent pull inviting you on a journey only seekers can experience.

THE KEY

At first, it's easy to dismiss. The mind offers reasonable explanations. Stress, too much coffee, lack of exercise, the changing seasons. But the stirring persists. It grows stronger until it becomes impossible to ignore.

Looking back now, I can see how the call had been building for months. But in that moment, standing in my kitchen on a Tuesday morning in late autumn, coffee mug halfway to my lips, something inside me simply stopped. Not my breathing or my heartbeat, but something deeper. The part of me that was blindly following daily routines came to a halt, straining to hear something beyond my awareness.

The kitchen looked exactly as it had the day before. Same countertops, same view, same stack of bills on the table. But everything felt different. Like I'd worn dirty glasses for years and someone finally cleaned the lenses.

In that moment of clarity, I saw my life as if from

above. I noticed the patterns, the routines, the careful ways I'd learned to stay safe and comfortable. While there was nothing wrong with any of it, there was also nothing particularly alive about it. I was existing rather than living. Maintaining rather than creating. Surviving rather than thriving.

The pull toward something more felt like a golden thread appearing in the corner of my vision. Faint but undeniable.

* * *

The Golden Thread

The call is not always dramatic. There are no burning bushes or divine revelations. Instead, there's a quiet but strong feeling that something is about to change.

It might come as a book that falls open to exactly the right page in a dusty corner of a shop you stepped into just to escape the rain. You might not remember the shopkeeper's face, but you remember how safe you felt standing there. A conversation that speaks directly to your soul. A dream so vivid it follows you into your waking hours. For me, it was simpler. A moment of such profound stillness,

I finally heard my heart's message.

The ancient wisdom keepers knew about this moment. They called it many things. The awakening, the stirring, the ascent. But they all understood that it marked the beginning of a journey from one way of being to another. From the familiar shores of who you have been to the uncharted territory of who you might become.

The thread that calls is golden not because of its color but because of its value. It is the thread that, when followed, leads you home to yourself. Following it requires courage. It means leaving behind the safety of the known for the uncertainty of what's beyond the gateway. It means believing in what lies beyond your current view and that you are capable of moving toward it.

When the call comes, place your hand over your heart and feel for the pull. Not the pull of obligation or expectation, but the pull of alignment. That deep resonance that says yes before your mind has time to say but.

This is your true north. Not a destination on a map, but a direction that feels right in your bones.

The call might arrive as a door closing. A relationship ending. A job that no longer fits. A health crisis that forces you to stop and reassess. It could also be a gentle feeling. A growing sense that life has more to offer, a desire for meaning that achievements or possessions can't satisfy.

This call is an invitation. Not a demand, but an offering. A chance to pass through the first gate of your transformation journey with the spark of desire.

As shocking as it sounds, this is where many stop. The call has come. The stirring inside has been felt. The golden thread has appeared, shimmering with possibility. But the choice to follow it requires something more. It means saying yes to uncertainty and change. You will also have to rethink what you believe about yourself and your life.

This is not easy. The familiar, even when uncomfortable, feels safer than the unknown. The patterns we've built, even when they no longer serve us, feel more secure than the open space of possibility. But here's what I learned at the first gate. Ignoring the call costs more than answering it.

When we ignore our feelings, push down our restlessness, and tell ourselves this life is good enough, something inside us starts to fade. Not all at once, but slowly. A dimming of the light. A quieting of the voice. A shrinking of the spirit. One day, we wake up and realize we've been living someone else's life. Following someone else's path. Pursuing someone else's dreams.

The tragedy is not that we failed. The tragedy is that we never tried.

You must understand that ignoring the call costs more than answering it does.

So I said yes. Not a loud, confident yes. Not a yes backed by certainty or a clear plan. It was a quiet, trembling yes that accepted a truth I couldn't ignore. Something needed to change, and that change had to start with me.

I didn't know where the path would lead. I didn't know what I would find or who I would become. I only knew I had to follow the thread. I had to step through the gate. I had to trust that the journey would show me what I needed to learn.

Here is where I learned something essential. I didn't have to do this alone. There is something larger than ourselves, a force that moves through all things. Some call it God. Some call it the Universe. Some call it the Tao, the natural order that flows through everything. I don't claim to know its name or nature, but I felt its presence.

When I said yes to the call, when I took that first trembling step, I felt held. Guided. As if my small courage had been met by something infinitely larger and more patient than I could comprehend.

You can always return. You can always pick safety over growth, comfort over change, the familiar over the unknown. But once you sense the call, once you spot that golden thread, once you glimpse the vibrant possibility of who you could be, you can never truly unsee it. The awareness has been planted. The seed has been sown. The only question is whether you'll water it or let it wither.

THE ANCHOR

The Stone

The golden thread itself becomes the anchor for the first gate. Not a literal thread, though some find one. More often, it's a symbol that represents the pull you felt, something that reminds you why you began this journey when the path gets difficult.

For me, it was a small stone I found on a walk the day after my kitchen revelation. Smooth and ordinary, the color of honey, it fit perfectly in my palm. I carried it in my pocket as a reminder. You said yes. Keep going.

Others have found their anchor in different forms. A bottle cap. A letter. A piece of jewelry. A quote written on a scrap of paper. The form doesn't matter. What matters is the meaning you give it.

The anchor serves a practical purpose. When doubt creeps in, when fear whispers that you should turn back, when the familiar calls you home, you have something tangible to hold. Something that says remember, you were brave enough to start. Be brave enough to continue.

THE PRACTICE

AWARENESS AUDIT (Body Sensing)

We spend most of our lives in our heads, rationalizing why we should stay stuck. The body, however, never lies. This practice helps you bypass the mind and locate your truth.

Stop. Find a quiet place where you can stand or sit uninterrupted.

Connect. Place your hand firmly over your heart. Close your eyes.

Locate. Do not look for a "message" or words. Scan your body for the physical sensation of "No" (contraction, heaviness, tightness in the gut) versus "Yes" (expansion, lightness, a deep breath).

Audit. Scan your last week. Recall a specific commitment or conversation. Did your body say "No" while your mouth said "Yes"?

FIELD NOTES

Use a separate journal to answer these prompts. Be honest. No one else needs to see this.

1. Pattern Recognition

List three moments in the last week where you felt a sudden, unexplained drain of energy. What were you doing? Who were you with? These are your "Anti-Calls."

2. The "Good Enough" Trap

Complete this sentence. "I am staying in this situation, job, or relationship not because I love it, but because I am afraid that _____."

3. Signal Detection

If your anxiety wasn't "bad," but was actually "excitement" without a place to go, what would it be excited about?

THE CROSSING

The invitation has come. The gateway is open. The path will become visible once you decide.

Will you follow it? Will you take the first step through?

The journey of transformation is not about becoming someone new. It's about remembering who you've always been beneath the layers of programming, expectation, and fear. These layers are where we find the gates of entry to the next level of growth. A level of soul expansion. The gates are not external places but barriers to internal passageways. Moments of clarity are the keys that cause the portals or passageways to be revealed. But only when you are ready to step through.

Are you ready?

This is your moment. Trust the process. Trust the journey. Trust the wisdom that brought you to this moment and will carry you through whatever comes next. Trust that you are not alone in this, that something greater moves with you, within you, supporting each step even when you cannot see the path ahead.

Find a small object at a crossroads or where two paths meet. A feather, a small trinket, or a pebble. Let it serve as your first Anchor. Hold it in your hand. Take a slow breath in through your nose, then exhale out your mouth for as long as you can. Whisper your "Yes" to the unknown.

Now, take a slow breath in through your nose, then exhale out your mouth for as long as you can.

The next gate requires your full commitment. But it also promises something the first gate could not. Depth. Truth. The kind of seeing that changes everything.

You have crossed the first threshold.

You are ready.

II

The Descent

This is where you're asked to dive beneath the surface of your life. Some call it "the dark night of the soul", shadow work, or an ego death. Either way, this is where you discover what has been lurking in the currents below your conscious mind. Stopping here will only anchor you in place, and trust me, you don't want to get stuck in the dark waters of your mind. Great courage is needed here. Know that the emotions that will arise are for your growth.

THE KEY

I learned about this descent the hard way, by trying to skip it entirely. Looking back now, I can see how naive that was. Imagining I could transform without facing what lived beneath the surface.

When I first felt the call to change my life, I thought transformation would be like redecorating a room. New paint, better furniture, maybe some inspiring quotes on the walls. I expected to upgrade my existing life. To become a shinier, more productive version of who I already was.

But transformation doesn't work that way. Real transformation requires diving below the surface to examine what lies beneath. To look at the currents that have been moving you unconsciously. To see which ones are carrying you toward your truth and which ones are keeping you stuck.

What comes up can be deeply uncomfortable.

The descent began for me with a simple question. Who am I when no one is watching?

I thought I knew the answer. I had been performing the role of myself for so long that I believed the performance was the truth. But in those fleeting moments between sleeping and waking, I noticed my thoughts. I observed how I reacted when I was by myself. It was then that I found someone I hardly recognized.

There was anger I hadn't acknowledged. Dreams I had buried so deep I'd forgotten they existed. Parts of myself I had deemed unacceptable and locked away in the dark.

There were patterns of behavior that had become so automatic I hadn't realized they were choices. Masks I had worn so long they had grown into my skin. A life I had built on the surface, while something else entirely lived in the depths below.

The Dark Waters

What appears at the second gateway looks like a mirror, but it's not like the ones we use to check our hair or straighten our clothes. This mirror is water itself. Dark, still, and impossibly deep.

In that moment, standing by the lake on a cool December evening, I saw it. The surface reflected everything. The bare trees, the gray sky, my own face staring back. But when I looked closer, past the reflection into the water itself, I saw darkness. Depth. Mystery.

Both exist at once. The reflection and the depths.

The surface and what lies below. This is the mirror of the second gate.

The water doesn't judge what it reflects or what it contains. It simply holds everything. The light and the dark, the surface and the depths, the reflection and the reality. And in that holding, it offers the possibility of seeing life-changing truth.

As I reflected on these deeper waters over the following weeks, I saw the ways I had been living. Living from fear disguised as practicality. Choosing approval over authenticity. Comfort over growth. Safety over adventure.

I saw the places where I had made myself shallow to avoid the depths. Where I had stayed on the surface because going deeper felt too risky, too uncertain, too real. I knew that if I went deep and others were not ready, I would be viewed negatively or even disowned.

Seeing at these depths was not comfortable.

There were nights when I ached to escape to the safety of the surface again. I questioned whether that pull toward something deeper was real or simply a whisper I made up, destined to fade if I ignored it long enough.

But something deep in me knew there was no going back. **You cannot unsee what you have seen. You cannot unknow what you have learned about yourself.** Once you've glimpsed the depths, the surface is never enough again.

Awareness is irreversible.
Once you see, you are responsible.

The descent, once begun, must be completed. If you turn away, you will likely repeat the same behavior patterns and revisit the same lessons. Eventually, you must acknowledge the reflection staring back and the darkness waiting below.

The last day of my vacation, by the lake that changed me, is when I felt it again. That pull toward the depths. Everyone around me was laughing, telling stories, playing cards near the water's edge. Some were gathering wood for a fire as dusk approached. The kind of moment that should have filled me with simple joy. But I found myself detaching, unable to fully be present. My mind kept drifting, questioning everything.

What was the point of all this? Why did life feel like we were all following a script someone else had written? Why did I feel like life is one big social experiment? Conditioned since childhood to want certain things, believe certain truths, follow certain paths.

I stared at the water while voices faded into background noise.

That's when I realized water changes depending

on the light that hits it. In harsh midday sun, it shows every ripple and imperfection with unflinching clarity, sometimes to the point of blindness. In soft twilight, it reveals gentleness, stillness, and mystery.

The gateway was not about which light to use, but to see yourself in all lights. To understand that you are not just one version of yourself, but many. That the person you are in moments of fear is as real as the person you are in moments of courage. That the self who feels lost is as valid as the self who feels found.

The lake was just the beginning. I spent months in these internal dark waters, looking at reflections I had been avoiding for years. I found myself staring into the shower stream, watching light reflect on the water. I'd watch the water spiral down the drain, carrying away more than just soap and shampoo. I stood in the rain on warm days, letting it wash over me like a baptism of truth. I tasted salt in my tears, knowing the release would wash away layers of the old.

Each form of water showed me something different.

The water teaches integration, not perfection. It shows you that transformation is not about becoming someone new, but about diving deep enough to discover who you've always been beneath the surface.

I began to understand why I had made certain choices. Why certain fears had such power over me. Why certain dreams had been abandoned and left to sink.

The water showed me the ways I had been living someone else's definition of success. The ways I had been performing as this happy person while feeling hollow inside. The ways I had been saying yes when I meant no, and staying silent when I needed to speak.

It showed me the child I had been before the world taught me to hide. The teenager who had learned that being different meant being alone. The young adult who traded authenticity for acceptance. The conditioning that told me to stay small, stay humble, stay quiet.

I learned that standing out meant danger. I understood that speaking up could bring consequences. People-pleasing became my survival strategy, and the fear of perception became my default setting.

But beneath all the masks, patterns, and protective layers, there was still something untouched. Something that had been waiting patiently for me to dive deep enough to find it. Like a pearl hidden in an oyster at the bottom of an ocean. A knowing that had never been lost, only submerged, waiting for me to stop skimming the surface long enough to recognize it.

The dark waters don't lie. They don't flatter. They don't soften the truth to make it easier to swallow. But they also don't condemn. They simply hold everything, offering you the chance to see yourself fully, perhaps for the first time in your life.

And in that seeing, something shifts. Not immediately. Not dramatically. But slowly, like water wearing away stone, the truth begins to reshape you. Drop by drop, wave by wave, the constant presence of what's real erodes what's false until something truer emerges.

You start to understand that the parts of yourself you've been hiding aren't weaknesses to be overcome, but aspects of your humanity to be integrated. That the anger you've been suppressing might be pointing toward boundaries you need to set. That the dreams you've been dismissing might be showing you the direction you need to walk.

The descent is not about fixing yourself. It's about seeing yourself clearly. All of yourself. Without judgment, without shame, without the need to immediately change or improve. Just seeing. Just knowing. Just being willing to stand at the edge of the dark waters and look at what they reflect, what they contain, what they reveal.

I learned to carry these waters with me as I moved deeper into this journey. Not literal water, but the practice of seeing, the willingness to look beneath the surface. Knowing how to acknowledge the depths, to stop pretending that what I showed the world was all that I was.

I started to feel less like a stranger in my own skin. No longer an imposter performing a role, but more like someone who was finally coming home.

The descent is not the easiest part of this journey, but it might be the most necessary. You cannot transform what you cannot see. You cannot change what you refuse to acknowledge. Most of all, you will not become who you're meant to be while still pretending to be someone you're not.

THE ANCHOR

The Coin

At the lake's edge, I saw something glinting in the mud. I dug it out, a tarnished silver coin, heavy and cold.

I scrubbed it clean in the lake water. One side was worn smooth from years of handling. This was the face I showed the world. The other side still held its sharp, intricate details, protected by the dirt. This was the truth of who I actually was.

I put it in my pocket next to the stone.

Your anchor for this gate is a coin. It represents the two sides of your existence. The performance and the reality. You must hold both to cross.

Some days I would hold it up to the light and watch how it changed depending on the angle. Other days I would simply touch it and remember. You have looked into the depths. You know what's there. You don't have to be afraid of it anymore.

Your anchor for this gate might be water itself, collected in a small container. Or it might be something else that represents depth to you. A mirror. A photograph taken at a meaningful moment. A stone from deep in the earth.

What matters is that it reminds you. You have descended, and you have survived. The depths did not consume you. They revealed you.

THE PRACTICE

Mirror Exposure

This practice uses the science of "mirror gazing" to disrupt your cognitive dissonance and help you integrate your shadow self.

Stand before a mirror in a private place.

Focus. Look directly into your own left eye. This is the eye linked to the right brain, the center of emotion.

Stay. Set a timer for 60 seconds. Do not look away. Notice the urge to flinch, to critique your appearance, or to leave.

Speak. Say out loud to your reflection. "I see you. I am not afraid of what is here."

Affirm. After confronting yourself, place your hand on your heart and speak words of acceptance. Say, "What I see here has value. No matter what has surfaced, I am worthy of love, belonging, and compassion." Let these words pour back into you. You have faced yourself. Now honor what you found.

FIELD NOTES

1. The Shadow Self

What is a personality trait you judge harshly in others? Examples might be, "They are so selfish," or "They are so lazy." Psychology tells us this is often a rejected part of ourselves. How do you secretly possess this trait?

2. The Cost Analysis

Write down the specific cost of keeping your "mask" on. Not just the emotional cost, but the actual cost. What specific opportunities, connections, or energy are you losing right now by pretending?

3. Cognitive Dissonance

Where are you performing a version of yourself that no longer exists? Perhaps "The Helpful One" or "The Easy-Going One." Name it.

THE CROSSING

The descent has stripped something away. You are raw, but you are real.

As you walked deeper into the second gate, you learned to breathe as you waded through the dark waters, no longer afraid of what they might reveal. The dark waters show you the truth, and the truth, however uncomfortable, is what sets you free.

But freedom comes with a cost. Once you've seen yourself clearly, once you've acknowledged what lived beneath, you cannot simply return to the surface and pretend nothing has changed.

In the days and weeks that followed, something unexpected happened. You felt lighter, yes, but also lost. The old certainties had dissolved. The familiar patterns had been exposed. You knew who you were no longer willing to be, but you didn't yet know who you were becoming.

Find a coin. Wash it clean. Hold it tight. Acknowledge that you are no longer willing to just skim the surface.

You have crossed the second threshold.

The third gate is opening. And it will teach you that before you can find your way, you must first become comfortable being lost.

III

The Wandering

This gate is the fog between who you were and who you're becoming. It unfolds as a sort of maze that operates on its own timeline, not yours. Here you'll learn how to move even when you can't see. To trust that stillness is a sacred pause and not the same as being stuck.

THE KEY

The descent had stripped something away, and I emerged from those dark waters feeling raw. Exposed. Like I'd shed a layer of skin and hadn't yet grown a new one.

For a brief moment, I felt like I was on higher ground. The kind of feeling you get when your chest expands after the thing weighing you down is finally lifted. The air felt thinner. Cleaner. Like standing on a mountain ridge at dawn, that first breath of cool air before the sun rises and the heat sets in. It was hope after renewal.

Then the sun came up, and I realized the cool air was just a pause between storms.

Within days, clarity slipped through my fingers. I found myself sitting in the parking lot of a coffee shop I'd driven to without knowing how I got there. I'd left the house that morning in early spring, focused and ready to tackle my to-do list. But between the third red light and the second car that swerved in front of me, my plans unraveled.

I sat there in my parked car, engine quiet, staring at the steering wheel. An unsettling fog clouded my thoughts. I had completely forgotten my purpose. Where was I headed? What was my next move?

The landscape around me looked familiar but felt foreign. Same streets. Same buildings. But something had shifted underneath. Like waking up in your own bedroom and not recognizing it for a moment. That split second of disorientation before your brain catches up.

Except my brain wasn't catching up.

I was lost in a place I'd lived for years. Not lost in terms of geography. I could find my way home. But lost in a way that felt irreparable. Every direction looked the same. Every choice felt pointless. The paths I was on, career, relationships, and daily routines, felt like they were going nowhere.

I had entered the gateway of the wandering.

The pull I felt that started this journey still whispered, but it was quieter now. At times, it would go silent for weeks or even months. In those moments of doubt, I discovered a grounding habit. I'd reach into my pocket and grasp the smooth stone I treasured. As I remembered sitting by the water, it reminded me of truths I held dear, anchoring me in the midst of uncertainty.

Before doubt and fear could take the wheel, I started the car. As a way to feel some sense of control, I'd drive home as my shield against the storms of the world. Yes, tomorrow awaited, but I knew if I could get home, I could rise one more time and face whatever came my way.

When Time Freezes

This maze I felt stuck in played with time in ways that made me question everything.

Some mornings I'd wake with energy and purpose. I'd make a cup of coffee and open my laptop, pull up my big project. The one that was supposed to change everything. Then, like clockwork, an hour would slip away, and all I'd done was scroll through emails. Gazing at the screen, disappointment settled in. What was wrong with me?

It wasn't depression. It was more specific than that. A paralysis that came from trying to force movement when the ground itself kept shifting.

I'd write three sentences and delete two. Start a task and abandon it halfway through. I had conversations that should have meant something, but I felt even more alone afterward.

I was doing things, but nothing was taking hold. The harder I tried to create momentum, the more stuck I became.

I wanted to control the pace, to decide when I'd learned enough and it was time to move forward. But the maze operated on different terms.

I'd feel ready to move and find myself frozen for another week. I'd feel completely unprepared and suddenly find an opening. By the time I gathered my things to move forward, I discovered the path had already changed. The opening I'd been waiting for had closed once again.

One afternoon, after a frustrating day of staring at screens and accomplishing nothing, I forced myself outside. Just to move. Just to breathe air that wasn't recycled through vents. To get some sunlight and maybe find inspiration in nature.

I walked without direction through a park near my house, past joggers and dog walkers and people who seemed to know exactly where they were going. I'd been collecting small things since the first gate. Rocks, feathers, anything that caught my eye and reminded me to stay present. Not all of them would travel with me, but I kept them within view at home.

That day, I almost didn't look down. I was rushing through my walk just to say I did it, not expecting to gain anything from it. But then something caught the light in the dirt where two paths crossed. I crouched down and brushed away the soil.

A small glass vial, half-buried, filled with sand. I picked it up and watched the grains shift and settle. It was like an hourglass without a frame. Time without structure. The sand didn't rush. It didn't resist. It just moved at the pace it moved, grain by grain, moment by moment.

It seemed like one of those geocache finds where someone left it for whoever was meant to find it. I slipped it into my pocket and continued my walk at a slower pace now.

This became my new reminder. I wasn't in charge of the timeline. I was in charge of how I moved through it.

Clarity does not arrive on command.
It arrives when the nervous system feels safe.

I could fight the pace and exhaust myself. Or I could trust that the wandering had its own rhythm. That preparation takes as long as it takes.

So I learned to be still. Not because I wanted to. Because I had no choice.

Other days brought chaos that made stillness feel impossible. I'd wake to a foggy mind, a swirling confusion that made every choice feel meaningless.

Questions I couldn't answer spun through my mind. What if I made a mistake? What if this path I followed was just confusion? What if there's nothing at the end of this?

I'd scroll through social media and see people who seemed to have it figured out. Who moved through the world with certainty and ease. Who posted about their wins, their growth, their transformation.

And I'd wonder what they knew that I didn't. What they had that I lacked.

The disorientation made me doubt everything. The journey. The call. Myself.

I tried to push through it with determination, with faith, with sheer stubborn will. But you can't fight your way out of a maze. You can only keep moving and trust that fog, by its nature, eventually clears.

I stumbled onto a video one sleepless night that changed my pace. It was someone talking about breathwork. About how changing your breathing could change your emotional state. It sounded too simple to work, but I was desperate enough to try.

I sat on my bedroom floor at 2 AM and followed the instructions. Breathe in for four counts. Hold for four. Out for four. Hold for four. Repeat for two minutes.

For the first few rounds, nothing happened. Just me, sitting on the floor, feeling ridiculous. My back hurt. I was uncomfortable. I couldn't focus. But I stuck with it, even for just a few rounds.

After a week or so, something shifted. Not dramatically. Just a slight loosening in my jaw and shoulders. A moment of space between the thoughts that brought peace.

I was able to hold it longer, sit up straighter, and stay present with the discomfort. It got easier, more natural. I noticed the change in my attitude and the way I responded when chaos was all around me.

I kept breathing.

For those few minutes, I wasn't lost. I wasn't confused. I was just here. Present. Breathing. Alive.

It didn't solve anything. But it gave me a place to stand when everything else was spinning. This practice made time slow down when I felt overwhelmed. It helped with the anxiety of everyday life and the racing thoughts that kept me up at night.

The wandering worked its magic like a patient sculptor. Not in sudden bursts, but with a steady hand carving away the excess clay, it revealed my spirit. I descended into nothingness. I later learned that ancient texts describe it as the key to the cycle of creation and destruction.

This is the breakdown before the buildup. The layers of self split apart to return to their original form. It resembles the old alchemical process. You need to completely dissolve something, letting go of its current shape, before you can change it into something new.

In that stripped-down state, something new began to form. I woke up one morning and realized I'd stopped comparing my progress to others. I'd even stopped feeling the need to perform for an invisible audience.

Those things had simply fallen away while I was focused on allowing the maze to do what it needed to do.

Yes, it was disorienting but survivable. What remained was simpler. Rawer. Truer.

The maze wasn't punishing me. It was preparing me for what would come next. During the wandering, it taught me patience, resilience, and the ability to keep moving when I couldn't see the point.

The wandering was ending. But the journey was far from over.

What waited ahead was different. A narrow entryway with the kind of intensity that doesn't just test endurance but solidifies what enters. I'd need to be lighter. Less weighed down by things that looked valuable but had no real substance.

The discomfort had become normal, something I could move through without panic. But what was up next was different. A kind of pressure I hadn't felt in a very long time.

It was as if the altitude was changing quickly. It got harder to take big breaths. My eyes watered so I couldn't see much ahead, just felt the heat coming closer.

I understood now why I'd learned to slow my breathing. Why the wandering had stripped me down and taught me to be still under pressure. Why I'd spent weeks learning to sit with the discomfort of the darkness.

It all made sense as I continued on the path toward

the portal that was opening, slowly revealing the gateway into the fire.

THE ANCHOR

The Sand

The glass vial filled with sand became the anchor for the third gate. I kept it on my desk where I could see it, a constant reminder that time moves at its own pace. That transformation cannot be rushed.

When impatience rose, when I wanted to force outcomes or skip ahead, I would pick up the vial and turn it in my hands. Watch the sand shift and settle. Remember that every grain matters. That the wandering, however frustrating, was doing its necessary work.

Your anchor for this gate might also involve time. A watch, an hourglass, a calendar marked with a significant date. Or it might be something that represents patience to you. Seeds waiting to sprout. A photograph of a tree that took decades to grow.

What matters is that it reminds you. Preparation takes as long as it takes. Divine timing operates on terms you cannot control. Trust the pace, even when it feels too slow or too fast.

THE PRACTICE

Box Breathing (Vagus Nerve Reset)

When you are lost, your nervous system scans for danger. This breathing technique manually switches your body from "Fight or Flight" to "Rest and Digest."

Inhale through your nose for a count of 4.
   Hold the breath at the top for a count of 4.
   Exhale through your mouth for a count of 4.
   Hold full exhaled for a count of 4.
   Repeat for two minutes.
   Do not judge yourself if your mind wanders. Just return to the count.

FIELD NOTES

1. Reframing Control

In the past, when things didn't go your way, did it eventually lead to something better? Write down one specific piece of evidence that a "delay" was actually a "protection."

2. Tolerance of Ambiguity

If you knew for a fact, with a 100% guarantee, that you would arrive safely at your destination in exactly 12 months, how would you enjoy today differently?

3. The Void

When you have nothing to do and the "fog" sets in, what do you reach for to avoid the silence? Phone, food, busy work? This is your numbing agent.

THE CROSSING

The wandering is ending. But the journey is far from over.

Before moving to the next gate, consider these questions:

Where in your life do you feel stuck or confused right now?

What would change if you trusted that being lost is part of finding your way?

What practice helps you stay calm when everything feels chaotic?

If you haven't already, begin a simple breathwork practice. Even two minutes a day. Notice what changes when you learn to regulate your own nervous system instead of waiting for external circumstances to calm down.

The wandering teaches you that transformation isn't linear. It's messy. Confusing. Full of wrong turns and backtracking. But every step, even the ones that feel pointless, is preparing you for what comes next.

Hold your sand or timepiece. Perform two minutes of Box Breathing. Accept that you are exactly where you need to be. You are ready. Even if you don't feel ready. Especially if you don't feel ready.

You have crossed the third threshold.

The fire is waiting.

IV

The Fire

This pathway squeezes from all sides,
asking only one question:
What matters most to you?

THE KEY

Sometimes, if you're lucky, the fire rises quietly at first, like heat rising from pavement after rain. The heat arrives disguised as daily pressure. Deadlines that demand decisions. Relationships that require more honesty than you've practiced. Opportunities that ask you to show up as someone you're still becoming.

In that moment, standing at my kitchen counter on a sweltering June morning, I encountered my fire. Three invitations had arrived within a single week. A job requiring relocation, a relationship demanding deeper commitment, and a creative project asking me to share work I'd kept hidden.

Separately, each felt manageable. Together, they created the perfect conditions for transformation. Heat, pressure, and no escape route but through.

These situations triggered every old pattern I thought I'd left behind. A critical email would land, and suddenly I was twelve years old again, desperate for approval. A difficult conversation loomed, and I found myself rehearsing the people-pleasing scripts I'd perfected over decades.

None of these situations seemed catastrophic on their own, but they stacked. One trigger pressed, then another, then another, until old beliefs about my worth, my capability, my right to take up space came flooding back with stunning force.

This is what the fire actually reveals. Not just what you're made of, but what you're still carrying. The situations themselves aren't too big. It's the weight of every unexamined belief, every inherited pattern, every outdated version of yourself that makes the heat unbearable.

You can't run from the fire that surrounds you. There's no exit strategy, no way to sidestep what's rising to the surface. You have to learn to move even when you're encircled by flames.

The fire never comes in the size you think you can handle. It arrives precisely when you've developed enough strength to discover what you're made of.

Here's what I learned about the fire that no one tells you. There are two ways to move through it, and both transform you completely. Your path depends entirely on what you learned during the wandering.

If you grasped the breathwork, if you practiced shifting your emotional patterns when intensity rose, if you truly integrated those lessons, you can move through the fire like a feather above the flames. Light enough to flow, grounded enough to feel the heat transforming you without being consumed by it. You stay present to the pressure, watching what rises to the surface when everything nonessential begins to burn away.

But if those lessons didn't quite take root, if you're still learning how to change your inner state when the world demands more than you think you can give, the fire will teach you differently. You'll need to get low. Crawl before you can walk again. The smoke will force you down to where the air is clearer, where humility becomes your guide. Everything you touch feels wrong. You can't see where you're going. The narrowness of the passage strips away every strategy that used to work.

Both paths lead to the same transformation. Both change you at the deepest level. The fire doesn't judge your method. It only cares about your willingness to be changed by what it reveals.

I tried the feather's path first. I had learned breathing techniques in the wandering, practices that helped me stay centered when chaos swirled around me. For a while, it worked. I could observe the pressure without drowning in it, feel the heat without being burned by it.

But there were moments, hours, sometimes days when the intensity overwhelmed my practice. When

I had to drop to my knees and crawl through the smoke, humbled and uncertain, trusting only that forward motion mattered more than graceful motion.

The fire taught me that transformation isn't about perfecting one path. It's about being willing to change, no matter how that change needs to happen.

Pressure's Purpose

I kept a small piece of coal on my desk during those weeks of impossible decisions. Raw, black, unremarkable. Some mornings I would hold it, feeling its weight and roughness, thinking about what happens when carbon faces unimaginable pressure deep in the earth.

The coal doesn't stay coal. Under enough heat and pressure, its molecular structure reorganizes completely. The carbon atoms arrange themselves into something crystalline, something that catches and reflects light in ways the original material never could.

The diamond isn't hidden inside the coal. The diamond is what the coal becomes when conditions demand transformation.

Pressure does not reveal who you are.
It forges who you become.

This is the most honest representation of what the fire stage demands. You are not uncovering something that was always there. You are becoming something new. The pressure doesn't reveal a hidden diamond. It creates one. It transforms the raw material of who you've been into something stronger, clearer, and more beautiful than you could have imagined.

You are being changed. Fundamentally. Completely. The fire doesn't just show you who you are. It transforms you into who you're meant to become.

The psychologist Carl Jung understood this process deeply. He wrote about how we must hold opposing tensions within ourselves until something entirely new emerges. You are simultaneously who you've been and who you're becoming. The fire is the space where both exist at once, where the old burns away and the new crystallizes into being.

This is not comfortable work. But it's necessary work. Every choice that feels too difficult, every situation demanding more than you think you can give, these are the forces that transform what you were into what you're becoming.

Water stripped away your illusions in the descent and showed you what lay beneath your surface. Heat does something different. It burns away the emotional reactions that no longer serve you and transforms what remains into something steadier.

Water cleanses your mind. Fire refines your emotional body.

The intense heat melts all the strategies and personas. The coping mechanisms that once helped you survive your old life may need to be refined as well. What seemed crucial in your previous existence loses its hold on you. Certain approvals, familiar securities, and the comfort of staying small. Not because you reject these things, but because they simply can't withstand the temperature of change.

This burning away feels like loss at first. Then you realize it's liberation.

You discover you can live without the approval you thought you needed because you're becoming someone who respects themselves. You can find security in uncertainty because you're developing something unshakeable within you. You can expand without losing yourself because you're finally becoming clear about what "yourself" actually means.

The shift happened gradually, then suddenly. I remember the morning I received another critical email, the kind that used to send me spiraling into self-doubt for days. I felt the familiar tightness in my chest, the old pattern rising to the surface. But this time, something was different.

I watched the reaction without becoming it. I felt the heat without letting it consume me.

It wasn't that the pressure had lessened. It was

that I had changed my relationship to it. The breathing techniques I'd practiced in the wandering finally clicked into place. I could stay present to the intensity without drowning in it. The external heat no longer created internal fire because I'd learned to regulate my own temperature.

That's when I understood. The fire wasn't just testing me. It was teaching me to handle heat from the outside by mastering the fire within.

From that point forward, patterns I'd carried for decades began to evaporate under the heat of new demands. People-pleasing became impossible when I started valuing my own truth. Perfectionism became irrelevant when I cared more about authenticity than approval. Fear of failure became absurd when I realized the real failure would be refusing to become who I was meant to be.

The fire reveals your core values. Not the ones you inherited or adopted, but the ones that are actually yours. Under pressure, you discover what you'll protect and what you'll let burn. What you'll fight for and what you'll release. What matters enough to stand firm on and what was never really yours to begin with.

The wandering gave you space to clear your mind and see what actually matters. The fire solidifies that clarity into embodiment. You stop knowing what you value and start living it.

You are being refined by heat, transformed by pressure, forged by intensity into someone who knows what they stand for.

THE ANCHOR

The Coal

The small piece of coal became the anchor for the fourth gate. Rough, messy, and potential-filled.

I placed it next to a small, clear quartz crystal. Not a diamond, but close enough. A reminder that transformation is real. That pressure creates beauty. That I had survived the fire and emerged changed.

Your anchor for this gate might be something that represents transformation to you. A before-and-after photograph. A piece of pottery that went through the kiln. A phoenix symbol. Coal and crystal side by side.

What matters is that it reminds you. You have been through the fire. You have been refined. You are not who you were when you entered.

THE PRACTICE

The Grip (Stress Reducer)

You cannot think your way out of pressure. You must feel your capacity to endure it.

Take your Anchor, the small piece of coal or a rough stone.

Squeeze it in your hand as hard as you possibly can.

Hold for 30 seconds. Feel the discomfort. Feel the intensity.

Notice that the pressure is intense, but you are separate from it.

You are the one holding. You are not the one being crushed.

Release. Watch the sensation fade. You can endure pressure without becoming it.

FIELD NOTES

1. Values Clarification

If you lost everything external tomorrow, your job, title, and house, what is the one thing about who you are that could not be taken away?

2. The Burn

What belief about yourself is currently being burned up by your circumstances? Perhaps "I'm not ready," or "I'm too old," or "I'm too broken." Name it.

3. Differentiation

Who are you trying to please right now? If they were disappointed in you, but you were proud of yourself, would you survive?

THE CROSSING

The fire has done its work. The pressure has transformed you. Now comes the crucial part. Standing firm in what you've become long enough for it to solidify.

Like coal under pressure, you must stay in the heat until the new structure is fully formed. Leave too soon, and you'll revert to old patterns. Stay present to the process, and you'll emerge as someone fundamentally changed.

You emerge from the fire not unscathed but unashamed. Not unchanged but clear about what has changed. Your core values, your essential nature, your true north. You have learned to trust yourself under pressure, to maintain your integrity in intensity, to stay soft in your heart even when you need to be strong in your stance.

The coal has become a diamond. Not in perfection, but in clarity. You can see through situations that used to confuse you because you know what you value. You can cut through complications that used to entangle you because you know what matters. You can reflect light in ways you never could before because you've been transformed into something that catches and holds and radiates truth.

As the fire begins to cool, you stand in the aftermath of your own becoming. The person who entered this gate no longer exists. In their place stands someone who has been tested by heat and emerged stronger. Someone who has felt old patterns burn away and new ones crystallize. Someone who has discovered that their worth isn't something to be proven but something to be embodied.

You look back at the narrow passage you crawled through, the flames that surrounded you, the moments you thought you couldn't continue. And you realize the fire wasn't trying to break you. It was remaking you.

Every trigger that surfaced old wounds, every pressure that demanded new responses, every moment you had to choose between who you were and who you're becoming, all of it was necessary.

The diamond has formed. Clear, strong, unbreakable in ways the coal never could have been.

This is a declaration of identity shifting. You are leaving the old definition of yourself behind.

Stand in a doorway in your home, a literal threshold.

Hold your Anchor, the coal or rough stone.

Step through the doorway consciously.

Speak your declaration aloud as you step.

"I am no longer the one who needed permission. I am now the One Who Chooses."

Or speak this truth. "I am my authentic self unapologetically."

Hold your coal or stone. Acknowledge the part of you that has burned away.

Welcome the diamond that is forming.

You have crossed the fourth threshold.

Ahead, the fifth gate beckons. Integration awaits. The profound work of bringing all these pieces together, of learning to live as this transformed version of yourself in a world that still remembers who you used to be. But that's the next passage.

For now, you stand in the cooling embers of your own becoming, feeling the certainty of what you've been transformed into, knowing with absolute clarity that you are ready for what comes next.

The fire has done its work. You have become.

V

The Closing

There comes a moment in every transformation when you realize you have arrived somewhere you have never been before, and yet it feels like the most familiar place in the world.

THE KEY

What has been learned now asks to be lived.

In that moment, waking up on an ordinary Tuesday morning in late summer, six months after emerging from the fire, something had shifted. The room looked the same. The sounds outside my window were familiar. But I felt different in my own skin, like I'd crossed into a new timeline overnight.

I knew it hadn't happened overnight at all. It had taken the entire journey to hold the alignment long enough to fully embody it.

My mind had gotten there first, understanding the truth of who I was. Then my emotions caught up, feeling safe enough to trust it. Now, finally, my physical reality was reflecting it back to me.

I moved through my morning, making coffee, the same routine that had marked the beginning of this journey. But everything felt different. The weight of the mug in my hand. The warmth spreading through my chest. The quality of light coming through the kitchen window. Everything was more vivid, more present, more real.

When I caught myself in the bathroom mirror, I stopped. Not startled, but drawn deeper. I could look into my own eyes now with a different under-standing, a different resonance. The person looking back at me was not performing or protecting or pretending. She was simply present. Simply real. Simply home.

I realized in that moment that I had been carrying a low-level tension for most of my adult life. The tension of trying to be acceptable, trying to fit in, trying to be who I thought I should be rather than who I actually was. And that tension was gone.

I could see it physically now. The inflammation in my face had softened. The puffiness around my eyes had disappeared. Even my posture had changed. The weight I'd been carrying in my shoulders had released. My body was finally relaxed, finally at ease, finally home in itself.

Devotion

That afternoon, something pulled me toward a small bookstore I'd passed a hundred times without entering.

The smell hit me first. Old paper and something else. Amber, maybe. Cedarwood. Something warm and grounding that made my chest expand. I wandered through narrow aisles until I found myself in a back corner where an elderly woman sat at a small table, her hands working over what looked like handmade jewelry.

"I wondered when you'd find your way here," she said without looking up.

I should have been startled, but I wasn't. Everything felt like it was unfolding exactly as it should.

She held up a simple silver ring, turning it in the light. Her eyes met mine with a warm smile, and she nodded for me to take it. "Try this one."

I hesitated. I'd never been one for jewelry, especially rings. But something about this one felt different.

It slid onto my finger like it had been waiting there. A perfect fit.

"That ring," she said, "is a symbol of devotion. Not to another person, but to yourself. To the truth of who you are. Most people spend their whole lives looking for someone else to complete them. This ring reminds you that you are already whole."

I lost my breath. That morning's realization, the recognition of my own wholeness, had led me here. The alignment was so precise it felt like magic.

"I have something else for you," she continued, "but I'll need to bring it tomorrow. It's part of my personal toolkit. Something that's gotten me this far in life. I only share it with people who are ready for it. Come back, and I'll have it waiting."

I left with the ring on my finger, though I knew some days I'd wear it on the necklace I never took off. Either way, it would stay with me. A reminder of completion. Of integration. Of remembering.

Over the following weeks, I watched the shift ripple outward into my environment. People responded to me differently, though I couldn't quite name what had changed. Conversations went deeper faster. Strangers shared things they "never tell anyone." Opportunities aligned with uncanny timing.

It wasn't that life became perfect. It was that I became present enough to recognize the perfection that was already there. When I slowed down enough to watch, I could see it. The way everything connected.

Challenges arrived exactly when I had developed the capacity to meet them. Losses cleared space for what was trying to emerge. What once looked like random chaos now revealed an underlying order I'd been too distracted to notice.

This recognition didn't come as an intellectual understanding but as a felt sense of rightness, of being exactly where I belonged in the vast web of existence.

I discovered that all the parts of myself I thought

were incompatible could actually coexist in beautiful harmony. My sensitivity didn't cancel out my strength. My creativity didn't undermine my practicality. I could crave solitude on Tuesday and deep connection on Wednesday without being inconsistent or broken.

I didn't have to choose. I could embody them all. **Wholeness didn't mean perfection.** It meant integration. It meant being large enough to contain all of my contradictions, wise enough to see how they complemented each other, and peaceful enough to let them dance together.

Being sensitive made me intuitive, not weak. Being strong made me reliable, not hard. I was not one thing or another. I was everything I had ever been, integrated into something greater than the sum of its parts.

The return brought a quiet kind of mastery. I got comfortable with questions. Mistakes became information instead of evidence of failure. I started trusting the unfolding instead of white-knuckling every outcome.

This mastery was really self-love. A deep nurturing that revealed itself outwardly. I felt like my true self again. I could shine in a way that showed others it was okay to answer their own calls. That it was worth it if they really wanted it.

I became myself in a world that often rewards

conformity. I stayed soft in situations that invited hardness. I made choices that felt true even when they weren't easy.

And something shifted. I stopped just witnessing the magic and started being it.

I poured into others without depleting myself. I left behind small gifts. A book. A note. A moment of full attention. They felt like anchor objects for people who were just beginning their own journeys. I held space for certain conversations. I checked in when I felt the call moving through me. I showed up when something whispered that I was needed.

People began to see me differently. Not as someone who had it all figured out, but as someone who had walked through fire and emerged with something worth sharing. They asked questions I didn't know I had answers to. They told me their stories, and something in me knew exactly what they needed to hear.

Perhaps the most beautiful aspect of the return was discovering that becoming fully myself was not a selfish act but a generous one. When I stopped trying to be who others wanted me to be and started being who I actually was, I gave everyone around me permission to do the same.

My authenticity became a gift to a world full of people wearing masks they'd forgotten they were wearing. My courage to be real inspired others to risk being real. My willingness to be vulnerable created space for others to drop their armor.

I discovered that the service I came here to provide could only be given when I showed up as who I actually was. My unique combination of gifts, wounds, experiences, and insights created a medicine that only I could offer. The world needed what I had, but it could only receive it when I stopped trying to give what I thought it wanted and started offering what I actually had.

This was the completion of the journey. The return to myself. The integration of all I had learned and become.

I was home.

THE ANCHOR

The Ring

The ring on my finger became the anchor for the fifth gate. Simple, silver, a circle with no beginning and no end. A reminder of wholeness. Of completion. Of devotion to myself.

Some days I would touch it and remember the woman in the bookstore, the way she'd looked at me like she knew something I was only beginning to understand. Other days I would simply feel its weight and know. You are home. You are whole. You are exactly who you're meant to be.

Your anchor for this gate might also be something circular. A ring, a bracelet, a stone with a hole through it. Or it might be something else that represents wholeness to you. A mandala. A photograph of yourself truly happy. A mirror that reflects you back to yourself with love.

What matters is that it reminds you. The journey has brought you home. Not to a new place, but to yourself. Finally, fully, completely.

THE PRACTICE

The Threshold

This is a practice of identity shifting. You are leaving the old definition of yourself behind.

Stand in a doorway in your home, a literal threshold.

Hold your Anchor, the ring or circle.

Step through the doorway consciously.

Speak your declaration aloud as you step.

"I am no longer the one defined by old patterns. I am now the One Who Chooses."

Or speak this truth. "I am my authentic self unapologetically."

Examples of declarations you might use:

"I am no longer the People Pleaser. I am now the One Who Chooses."

"I am no longer the Victim. I am now the Creator."

"I am no longer the Fixer. I am now the Guide."

FIELD NOTES

1. Evidence of Change

List three small things you did differently this week that the "Old You" would never have done.

2. Identity Shifting

Complete this sentence. "I used to be the kind of person who _____, but now I am the kind of person who _____."

3. Wholeness

What "contradiction" do you love about yourself now? For example, "I am soft but I have steel boundaries."

THE CROSSING

You are not just completing a journey. You are becoming a light for others to follow. As you stand at the threshold of the fifth gate, ask yourself:

What does "home" feel like in your body right now?

What parts of yourself are you finally able to accept?

How can you share your wholeness with others instead of hiding it?

The return is not about perfection. It's about presence. It's about being so fully yourself that others feel permission to be themselves too.

Put on your ring or hold your circle. Step through your doorway. Welcome yourself home. You have crossed the fifth threshold.

And yet. As you settle into this new way of being, as the ring of devotion becomes familiar on your finger, you begin to notice something. A subtle shift in the air. A quality of attention that feels almost like being watched, but not by anything outside yourself.

The next day, I returned to the bookstore. That same warm, grounding scent wrapped around me as I stepped inside. The woman was waiting, a small wrapped package on the table in front of her.

"Tomorrow," she said with a smile, "you'll understand why this matters."

VI

The Integration

This gate holds the final key. The one that seals everything you've walked through to mark the completion of your journey. It's time to step fully into the truth of who you've become and get a glimpse of what waits on the other side.

THE KEY

I had almost forgotten about the bookstore.

How could I forget the woman with silver-streaked hair pulled back in a loose bun, wearing a linen apron over jeans and a soft gray sweater, who had looked at me like she recognized something familiar? Not because she could see the future, but because she'd walked a similar path herself.

My feet remembered the way. They carried me through familiar streets on that crisp autumn morning until I caught it again. That scent. Warm and grounding, like earth after rain mixed with lavender and something citrusy. Something that made my nervous system settle without understanding why.

The door chimed as I entered. The scent was stronger here, wrapping around me like a familiar embrace. My shoulders dropped. My breath deepened. Something in my body remembered this place even though my mind had let it go.

She was there, behind the counter, organizing a display of small amber bottles. Essential oil blends she made herself, I realized now. When she looked up, her face broke into a smile that reached her eyes.

"You're back," she said. Not surprised. Just acknowledging.

"I am."

She studied me for a moment, the way someone who's been through their own transformation studies another person going through theirs. "Then you're ready."

"Ready for what?"

Instead of answering, she reached beneath the counter and pulled out a small package wrapped in brown paper and tied with twine. She placed it on the counter between us.

"I told you I'd have something for you," she said. "When you were ready."

The package was smaller than my palm, light as air. I stared at it.

"What is it?"

"A tool," she said simply. "The first one for your kit. You'll need it where you're going."

"Where am I going?"

Her smile was gentle. "Into the work of guiding others through their own transformation. Into holding space for those who are ready to change. I've been doing this work for fifteen years. I recognize the shift that happens when someone's about to step into that role."

My hand moved toward the package, then hesitated. "I don't understand."

"You will." She pushed it closer. "This is the blend you've been smelling since you first walked in here. I make it myself. It's more than just scent. It's a tool that helps you come back to yourself when safety and security seem out of reach or things get overwhelming. When you're at a threshold, not sure what step to take next."

I picked up the package. It felt alive in my hand, as if it held something waiting to be awakened. "How do I..."

But when I looked up, she had already turned away, moving toward a customer who had just entered. Her attention shifted naturally, the way someone who runs a business shifts between conversations.

The message was clear. This was my moment. My choice. My next step.

I slipped the package into my pocket and walked outside.

The Reset Kit

It was late afternoon, and I had to leave this small town to head back to the city. As I got in my car, the sun painted everything gold, reflecting off the rearview mirror as I settled into my seat and grabbed the small package.

My fingers worked at the twine, careful not to tear the paper. Inside was a small amber bottle, no bigger than my thumb. The glass was old, hand-blown, with tiny imperfections that caught the light. A label wrapped around it, handwritten in careful script.

For returning to true north when the world tilts sideways.

On the back, instructions.

Place a drop on your palms. Rub together. Cup your hands over your nose and breathe.

I uncapped the bottle. The scent rose up immediately. That same grounding, centering fragrance from the bookstore, but more concentrated. More alive. Like breathing in the essence of coming home.

Following the instructions felt natural. A drop on my palms. I rubbed them together. The warmth of my skin releasing the scent. My hands cupped over my nose. And then, the breath.

Everything shifted.

Not dramatically. Not like a lightning bolt or a revelation. Just a gentle settling.

A return. A remembering.

My nervous system relaxed. I hadn't realized I was still carrying the residual tension of the day. The rush to finish everything before heading home, the weight of returning to my regular routine. But now it all released. My thoughts, which had been spinning with questions about what came next, quieted.

And in that quiet, I felt it.

The opening of the veil. This was like a higher view of everything, but in a detached way. One where I wasn't overthinking going back to work tomorrow or the traffic I'd run into tonight on the way home, but a view of the bigger picture and connectedness of it all.

The oil wasn't magic. It was a tool. A practical, tangible anchor that helped my body remember what my mind sometimes forgot. That I could return to center. That I could access the knowing that lived beneath the noise. That I could stand at the edge of the unknown and trust what I couldn't see.

This was the last key I needed for my kit.

Not a key that opened a single door, but a tool that helped me think clearly when clarity mattered most. One that brought me back to myself when the world tried to pull me in a thousand directions.

Time passed as I sat there, breathing. Centering. Remembering.

When I finally opened my eyes, the sun had dropped lower. But I felt grounded. Ready.

I reached into my bag and pulled out the worn leather pouch, loosening the drawstring. One by one, I laid the objects on the passenger seat beside me.

The honey-colored stone that started it all. Smooth and solid, the weight of saying yes when I didn't know what I was saying yes to. The decision to begin.

The coin from the lake. The descent that taught me to see beneath the surface, to acknowledge the depths without fear.

The vial of sand from the maze. Each grain a reminder that transformation happens slowly, that divine timing operates on terms I couldn't rush or control. Patience when I wanted answers.

The small piece of coal, still rough in my palm. The fire that refined me, the pressure that revealed what I was made of. Proof that I could withstand the heat and emerge changed.

The ring on my finger caught the fading light. Integration. Wholeness. The closing that made me real in my own skin.

And now this. The small bottle of oil. The tool that would bring me home to myself when the world pulled me away. Clarity when I needed it most.

I looked at them together, these anchors from each gate, and understood something I hadn't seen before. Each one had prepared me for the next. The stone gave me the courage to descend. The descent taught me to see. The seeing prepared me to wander without losing myself. The wandering built the patience and breath I needed to survive the fire. The fire refined me enough to integrate. And the integration made me steady enough to step beyond the veil.

Each gate had given me exactly what I needed for what came next.

I gathered them carefully and returned them to the pouch, then placed the bottle beside it in my bag. My reset toolkit. The beginning of something I didn't fully understand yet but knew I would need.

The bookstore woman had known. Somehow, she had known exactly what I would need and exactly when I would be ready to receive it.

As I drove by the bookstore, I could see the same lady who believed in me helping other customers, her hands moving with the same gentle certainty she had shown me.

How many others had she given tools to? How many seekers had walked through that door, drawn by a scent they couldn't name, and walked out with exactly what they needed for their journey?

The answer didn't matter because now I understood something deeper. The work wasn't just about my own transformation. It was about learning to hold space for others. About gathering tools that could help not just me, but anyone who was ready to walk through their own gates.

THE ANCHOR

The Scent

The amber bottle of oil became the anchor for the sixth gate. I kept it in my bag, always within reach. A tool that could bring me back to center when the world tried to pull me away.

Your anchor for this gate might also be a scent. Essential oil, a favorite perfume, and incense that grounds you. Or it might be something else that brings you back to yourself. A photograph, a sound, a texture that reminds you of home.

What matters is that it helps you return. To center. To clarity. To yourself.

THE PRACTICE

Scent Anchoring

You are conditioning your brain to associate this scent with safety.

Apply the scent to your palms.

Rub your palms together.

Cup your hands over your nose.

Breathe deeply for 30 seconds.

Repeat this every time you feel safe, calm, or happy.

Use it when you are stressed to physically lower your cortisol and return to center.

FIELD NOTES

1. The Ripple Effect

Who is watching you right now? Children, friends, colleagues? What permission are you giving them by living authentically?

2. Service

If your pain was actually training for a future role as a guide, what are you now qualified to teach?

3. The Next Threshold

What is the specific action or decision you feel pulled toward right now, even if it scares you?

THE CROSSING

A week later, I was sitting in a coffee shop when I saw her.

She was young, maybe mid-twenties, with the kind of restless energy that comes from knowing you're supposed to be somewhere but having no idea where. At the table next to mine, she stared at her laptop screen without really seeing it. Her fingers drummed against the table in an unconscious rhythm.

That rhythm was familiar. I had drummed it myself, months ago, in another life.

She looked up and caught me watching. "Sorry," she said, stilling her hands. "Nervous habit."

"No need to apologize. I know that feeling."

She smiled, but it didn't reach her eyes. "Yeah? What's the cure?"

The question hung in the air. The gates and the keys and the journey that had changed everything flooded my mind. The bookstore woman and the amber bottle now living in my bag.

"There's no cure," I said finally. "But there are tools. And a path."

She tilted her head, curious now. "What kind of path?"

The small notebook I had been carrying came out of my bag. Inside, I had been sketching a map of my journey, each gate marked with symbols and notes only I understood. I hadn't known why I was drawing it until this moment. Now the reason was clear.

I tore out the map and slid it across the table.

She picked it up, studying the lines and symbols. Then looked at me with questions in her eyes. "What is this?"

"A beginning. If you want it to be."

She stared at the paper for a long moment. Her fingers had stopped drumming. Her breathing had slowed. Something in her was recognizing something in the words, even if she didn't understand it yet.

"There's a way, a path that life takes you on sometimes expectedly and sometimes unexpectedly." I slowly pulled back my enthusiasm. "We can reach the destination we're seeking, wherever that is for you, but only by walking the way."

The young woman folded the paper carefully and slipped it into her pocket. When she looked at me again, her eyes were different. Clearer. More present.

"In life we get caught up in the everyday things. Sometimes we miss what's already there. There are answers all around us, we just have to be able to hold space for them. The true work comes with the follow-through, the action to get to where we want to go."

She said, "That's my issue. I don't know where I want to go or what to do next. It feels like everything is happening all at once."

I shook my head, reached in my bag, and handed her the small bottle. "This might help you figure out the next step. The map kind of comes alive when paired with this. Things reveal themselves in the right time."

"Thank you," she said.

Gathering my things, I stood to leave. This was how it worked. Not hoarding the knowledge. Not keeping the tools to myself. But learning to recognize when someone was ready and offering them a thread to follow.

The golden thread I had followed was now becoming threads I could offer to others.

Outside, the air was crisp and clear. The sun was hitting its peak and the warmth slowly blanketed my body. My feet started moving, not toward anywhere in particular, just forward, into whatever came next.

The gates are always opening.

For those who are ready to walk through them.

For those who trust the call.

The gates taught me to trust the process. The keys taught me to carry what matters. The guide taught me to move when I feel the call. And now, my toolkit shows me something new. That transformation isn't just internal. It's practical. Tangible. Something you can hold in your hand and carry with you into the world. You also don't have to go at this alone. We are actually needed to assist the next person.

What door will open next remains unknown but I'm ready to find out. And when I do, I'll have the tools I need to walk through it.

Somewhere, someone else is catching a scent they can't name and following it toward their own transformation.

The veil is thin. The tools are ready. The work begins.

As you stand at the threshold of the sixth gate, ask yourself:

Who might need what you've learned?

What would it look like to share your journey without forcing it?

What tool or practice helps you return to yourself when life gets chaotic?

The hidden gate teaches you that transformation is never just for you. It's for everyone your life touches. Every person you meet. Every conversation you hold. Every moment you show up as who you actually are.

You are becoming a guide. Not because you have all the answers, but because you've walked the path and can light the way for others. Now it's time to share what you have learned.

Apply your scent.

Breathe.

Step forward.

You have crossed the final threshold.

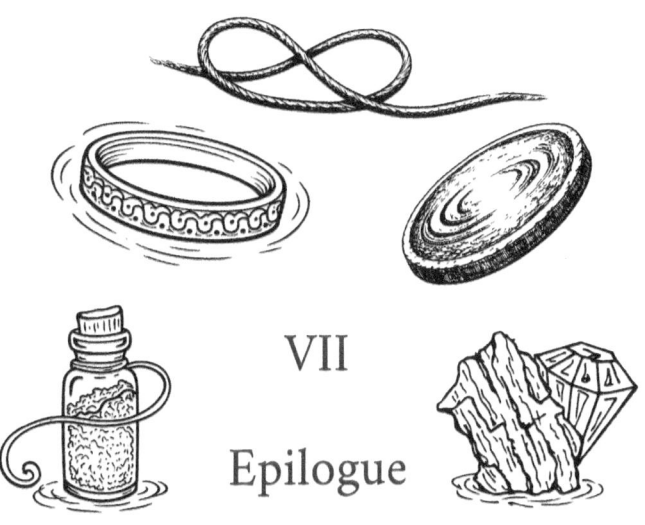

VII

Epilogue

*The way of the seeker is a journey not many
are bold enough to walk, and yet here you are.*

THE JOURNEY CONTINUES

One year later, I'm sitting in my favorite bookstore, tucked into a corner chair. I reach into my bag and pull out a small leather journal. One of several I keep with me now. Inside the front cover, I've written a single question.

What if everything you need is already with you?

A stranger settles into the chair beside me, and something about her reminds me of myself a year ago.

She has that look. The one I recognize immediately now. Eyes searching. Hands fidgeting with her cup. That restless energy that comes right before everything changes.

She glances at my journal, then at me. "Sorry, I don't mean to interrupt. It's just, do you ever feel like you're supposed to be doing something different with your life, but you have no idea what?"

The question hangs in the air between us. I close my journal and turn to face her fully.

"All the time," I say. "Or at least, I used to."

She laughs nervously, relief washing over her face. "I don't know why I'm asking a complete stranger this. You probably think I'm crazy."

I smile because I remember saying those exact words. I remember the desperation of the 3 AM Google searches. The spiritual books that promised transformation but delivered only concepts. The false starts and dead ends. The teachers are performing enlightenment rather than embodying it.

"You're not crazy," I tell her. "You're being called."

The transformation didn't make me perfect. There were still mornings I woke up and fell into old patterns. People-pleasing in a conversation, second-guessing a decision I knew was right, feeling that familiar tightness when someone's approval seemed to slip away. But now I could see it happening. I'd catch myself mid-performance and pause. Sometimes I'd choose differently in the moment. Other times, I'd only notice afterward, but even that noticing was progress. The difference wasn't that I never stumbled. It was then that I no longer stayed down.

My leather pouch sits in my bag, heavier now than when the journey began. Inside are the original anchors. The honey-colored stone from Gate 1 that taught me to say yes, the coin from Gate 2 that taught me to see beneath the surface, the vial of sand from Gate 3 that taught me patience, the small piece of coal from Gate 4 that reminds me transformation requires pressure, the ring from Gate 5 that symbolizes wholeness, and the amber bottle of oil from Gate 6 that brings me back to presence.

I still reach for them. The stone when I need courage to begin something new. The coin when I need to look deeper. The sand when I'm rushing and need to remember divine timing. The coal when I'm in the middle of something hard and need to trust the refining process. The ring when I forget I'm already whole. The oil when the world pulls me away from myself and I need to come home.

But the pouch has grown. New objects have found their way in as the work of guiding others has evolved. A small shell from a beach walk with a client who was learning to trust the ebb and flow of her own cycles. An acorn from the park where I sat with someone navigating their own descent, reminding them that mighty things grow from small beginnings. A coin given to me by a woman who said our conversation was worth more than any therapy session. I carry it as a reminder that this work has value, that I don't have to diminish what I offer.

Each new object represents someone else's journey intersecting with mine. Each one a reminder that the gates keep opening, that the work continues, that transformation is both deeply personal and endlessly collective.

The original anchors are still the foundation. They're what I return to when I lose my way, what I offer to others when they ask how to begin. But the new tools show me something important. The journey doesn't end when you walk through the gates. It expands. It deepens. It becomes something you carry forward and share.

But the real toolkit isn't in my bag. It's in my practice.

I write almost every night. Some weeks it's more often than others. When I feel myself holding on to more emotional and mental weight than I can hold, I know it's time to let it out on paper. The pages have become mirrors, showing me patterns I couldn't see when they were just thoughts spinning in my head. Some days I write about gratitude. Other days, I write about resistance. Both are equally valuable. Both are part of the journey.

I've learned that transformation isn't a destination you reach. It's a practice you return to. Again and again. Each time you move through a gate, you don't leave it behind. You integrate it. You carry it with you. The call becomes a compass. The threshold activates courage. The shadow becomes wisdom.

And then, when you're ready, you realize something profound. You're not just walking the path anymore. You're becoming the path for others.

I didn't plan to become a guide. It happened naturally, the way all true callings do. People started noticing something different about me. Not that I had all the answers, but that I was comfortable with the questions. Not that I'd arrived somewhere, but that I was genuinely present wherever I was.

They started asking me about the changes they saw. The way I moved through challenges. The way I spoke about difficulty without making it dramatic. The way I seemed to trust something they couldn't quite name.

"What happened to you?" they'd ask.

And I'd tell them the truth. "I stopped running from myself. I started listening instead."

Some would nod and change the subject. But others, the ones who were ready, would lean in. Their eyes would light up with recognition. And I'd know they were hearing their own call.

Those are the ones I give the journals to. The ones I share the questions with. Not because I have their answers, but because I remember what it felt like to think I was alone in the searching.

You're never alone in this. **The journey of transformation is the most universal human experience there is. We're all being called. We're all crossing thresholds. We're all learning to trust the unfolding. The only difference is whether we answer.**

Last week, I ran into someone I gave a journal to six months ago. She looked different. Lighter. More present. She told me she'd filled three journals since then. That she'd started noticing her own patterns. That she'd made a major life change she'd been avoiding for years.

"It's like I can finally see," she said. "Not everything. But enough. Enough to take the next step."

That's when I knew. This work doesn't end. It expands.

Each person who answers their call becomes a light for others. Each person who moves through their gates opens those gates a little wider for the next person. Each person who finds their true north makes it easier for others to trust their own internal compass.

This is how transformation spreads. Not through grand teachings or perfect systems, but through ordinary people doing the extraordinary work of becoming themselves. Through quiet courage and honest questions. Through journals and conversations and moments of recognition. Through you.

The call has found you.
The gates are opening.
You are now ready.
Trust the journey.

THE DAILY PRACTICE

Transformation does not complete itself through insight alone. What you have learned must be integrated into the body, the nervous system, and daily life. Neuroscience shows that lasting change happens when awareness is paired with repetition, regulation, and choice. New neural pathways form not when you understand something once, but when you *practice responding differently over time*.

> *Integration is not about doing more. It's about being able to respond differently.*

When you slow your body down, your brain can make better decisions. When you repeat small actions, new habits form. When you choose differently in familiar moments, your identity begins to shift.

You don't need to remember everything in this book.

You only need to remember **how to return to yourself**.

The Three Anchors For Lasting Change

1. Regulation (Safety First) - *Change cannot be sustained in a dysregulated nervous system.*
When you feel overwhelmed, confused, or tempted to revert to old patterns, return to the breathwork you learned in *The Wandering*. Even two minutes can signal safety to the brain and allow higher reasoning to return.

Start with the Body

When you feel overwhelmed, confused, or pulled back into old patterns, begin here:
Slow your breathing.
Place one hand on your chest or stomach.
Take one slow breath in through your nose.
Exhale slowly through your mouth.
This tells your nervous system that you are safe.
A calm body creates a clear mind.
You don't need to fix the moment.
You need to steady yourself inside it.

A regulated body creates a clear mind.

2. Recognition (Pattern Awareness) - *Name Where You Are*
You now understand the stages of change.

When something feels intense, ask yourself:

- Am I hearing a **Call** to change?
- Am I in a **Descent**, facing something uncomfortable?
- Am I **Wandering**, unsure of the next step?
- Am I in the **Fire**, under pressure or making a hard choice?
- Or am I **Integrating**, learning how to live what I've learned?

Naming the stage helps your brain make sense of the experience. It reduces fear and reminds you that this is part of the process. You now know what to do when that gateway opens again.

When a moment feels intense, ask:
Which gate am I in right now?

3. Choice (Embodiment) - *Integration happens when you choose differently once, then again, then again. Not perfectly. Consistently.*

When faced with a familiar trigger, ask:

- What would the version of me who crossed the fire choose here?
- What anchor do I need to hold right now?

Small choices compound into identity.

A Simple Daily Integration Practice (2-3 minutes)

1. Place a hand on your chest
2. Take one slow breath in through the nose, out through the mouth
3. Then choose one small action that feels true:

- Speak honestly instead of staying silent
- Rest instead of pushing
- Say no instead of over committing
- Slow down instead of rushing to fix things

Transformation does not ask for urgency. It asks for presence.

* * *

Use Your Anchors

The objects you've collected are reminders, not symbols.

They are tools.

When you feel unsteady, hold one.

Let it bring you back to what you already know.

You don't need to figure everything out again.

You've already learned how to return.

114

A Simple Daily Check-In (2 Minutes)

Once a day, ask yourself:

- How does my body feel right now?
- What stage am I moving through?
- What is one small choice I can make today that supports who I'm becoming?

You don't need a perfect plan. You need presence. Integration doesn't mean life becomes easy. It means you become steadier. You will still face pressure. You will still feel unsure at times. The difference now is that you know how to pause, how to listen, and how to choose.

You are ready.

A LETTER TO THE SEEKER

What I've learned in this year of practice and witnessing is that you didn't find this book by accident.

You're reading these words because somewhere inside you, something is stirring. A restlessness. A knowing. A call that's been getting louder even as you've tried to ignore it.

You picked up this book because you're ready. Maybe you don't feel ready. Maybe you feel terrified or confused or completely unprepared. That's okay. That's actually perfect. Readiness isn't about having it all figured out. It's about being willing to begin.

The gates are already opening in your life. You might not recognize them yet, but they're there. In the dissatisfaction that won't go away. In the dreams that keep returning. In the moments when you catch yourself thinking, there has to be more than this. That's not discontent. That's your soul calling you home.

The keys are forming in your awareness right now. In the questions you're asking. In the patterns you're starting to notice. In the way these words are resonating with something you've always known but couldn't quite name.

The anchors are waiting to be discovered in your everyday life. In objects that suddenly feel significant. In practices that ground you. In the small ceremonies that remind you who you really are.

Everything you need is already around you. These pages have simply reminded you how to look.

So here's my invitation to you, fellow seeker. **Start where you are. Not where you think you should be. Not where others expect you to be. Right here, in this moment, with all your uncertainty and hope and fear and courage mixed together.**

Get a journal. Any journal. It doesn't have to be special. What matters is that you begin to witness your own unfolding on the page.

Ask yourself the questions that scare you. The ones you've been avoiding. The ones that don't have easy answers. Write them down. Sit with them. Let them work on you.

Notice what calls to you. What makes you feel alive. What makes you feel like yourself. Follow those golden threads, even when you can't see where they lead.

Trust the process. Trust the journey. Trust the wisdom that brought you to this moment and will carry you through whatever comes next.

And know this. The journey doesn't end here. This is just the beginning.

There are deeper gates ahead. More profound recognitions waiting. Levels of understanding and integration that will transform not just how you live, but how you experience being alive.

But those gates will open when you're ready for them. When you've done the work of these first six. When you've built your foundation strong enough to support the next level of your becoming.

For now, this is enough. Answer the call. Cross the threshold. Face your shadow. Find your true north. Claim your voice. Anchor your truth.

Do this, and everything else will unfold in its own perfect timing.

I slip my journal into my bag and run my fingers over the smooth shell in my pocket as I stand to leave the bookstore. How many people here are being called right now? How many are standing at their own thresholds, feeling that familiar restlessness, wondering if they're brave enough to begin?

More than I can see.

And somewhere, someone is reading these words and feeling something shift inside them. A recognition. A remembering. A readiness they didn't know they had.

That someone is you.

Welcome, seeker. Your journey is just begin-ning.

I can't wait to see where it takes you!
  T.L. Hurd

THE WAY OF THE SEEKER

GATE OPENINGS

GATE 1 - THE CALL
GATE 2 - THE DESCENT
GATE 3 - THE WANDERING
GATE 4 - THE FIRE
GATE 5 - THE CLOSING
GATE 6 - THE INTEGRATION

ABOUT THE AUTHOR

Tiffany Hurd is a guide for those ready to remember who they've always been beneath the layers of conditioning and fear. Through her work with Born Vital and personal brand under AlcheMentor, she helps seekers transform their relationship with themselves and step into their most authentic expression, helping them discover that transformation is not about becoming someone new, but about remembering who they've always been.

If these pages have stirred something in you, if you're ready to dive deeper into your own transformation, I invite you to explore the resources waiting for you.

BornVital.com

YouTube: @alchementorlab
Instagram: @alchementor
TikTok: @alchementor

Other Books by T.L. Hurd

5 Keys to Living a Successful Life
This book was written in a way to guide you through the beginning stages of a personal transformation. It will assist you in seeing growth in areas you have struggled in, as well as, in areas of importance to live a healthy, happy life.

Awaken Your Purpose: Find Clarity in Your Purpose
In this book secrets will be revealed on how to unlock your potential to find your purpose. Greatness will pour from you and doors of opportunity will open as you adapt the strategies given in this book.

"Having potential is imperative but at some point you have to unleash it!"

Decision Making the Easy Way: The #1 Strategic Thinking and Decision Making Hack
Learn how to understand time, the importance of your decisions, and how to make the right choices in any situation. After enough steps are built in the right direction you will stand at the door of opportunities and experience success.